Tax Secrets

For

The Smiling Retiree

BW

Navi J. Dowty, CFA

Copyright © 2019 Navi J. Dowty

All rights reserved.

No part of this book may be reproduced or transmitted in any form or by any means, electronic or mechanical, including photocopying, recording, or by any information storage and retrieval system, without permission in writing from the author.

First Printing 2019

First Edition 2019

9781798175163

Disclaimer

This book is presented solely for educational purposes and is not represented or intended for you to use as exhaustive tax advice. The information contained in this book is made available for illustrative purposes, explaining only the basics of tax planning.

I emphasize that the information contained in this book is not offered to you as financial, legal, accounting, or other professional services' advice. I highly recommend that you seek the services of a competent professional before making any decisions regarding your personal or business finances and taxes.

However, best efforts have underscored the writing of this book, but the author makes no representations or warranties of any kind and assumes no liabilities of any kind with respect to the accuracy or completeness of the contents and specifically disclaim any warranties of use for any particular purpose.

The author shall not be held liable or responsible to any person or entity with respect to any loss or incidental or consequential damages caused, or alleged to have been caused, directly or indirectly, by the information contained in this book, or disruption caused by errors or omissions, whether such errors or omissions result from negligence, accident, or any other cause.

Any case studies are fictional and any reference to actual persons, either living or dead, is completely coincidental. The tax case studies represented in this book were created to show only the highlights of how a taxpayer might choose to make tax planning decisions.

The reader is advised to consult with a professional tax advisor who has experience with guiding clients and making tax planning choices relevant to an individuals or companies financial and tax situation.

Any investment advice is offered thru Associated Retirement Planners, Inc.

This Book is for You

…if you are near retirement or in retirement now, or you want to know how to:

• Preserve your wealth

• Increase your income

• Avoid high taxes

• Stay Ahead of Inflation

• Use interest rates to your advantage

This book reveals some of the tax secrets every Smiling Retiree needs to know!

NDA
Navi Dowty and Associates, Inc.

Navi Dowty & Associates, Inc.

Associated Retirement Planners, Inc.

Associated Retirement Planners, Inc. is a

Registered Investment

Planners, Inc.

Returns sited are just hypothetical examples and are not guaranteed.

Navi Dowty & Associates, Inc.

Associated Retirement Planners, Inc.

290 S. County Farm Rd, Ste. P

Wheaton, IL 60187

630-893-4142

And,

Navi Dowty & Associates, Inc.

Associated Retirement Planners, Inc

1102 Grand Avenue

Wausau, Wisconsin 54403

715-845-4367

www.NaviDowty.com

TABLE OF CONTENTS

FOREWORD I
INTRODUCTION IV
CHAPTER 1 1
HOW TO THINK ABOUT YOUR TAXES
CHAPTER 2 16
TAXES ARE MYSTERIOUS
CHAPTER 3 26
TAXES ARE ON SALE
CHAPTER 4 28
THE QUESTION IS WHAT HAPPENS NEXT?
CHAPTER 5 30
SAVING TAXES RIGHT NOW
CHAPTER 6 54
HOW ABOUT BUSINESSES
CHAPTER 7 58
PAY TAXES NOW
CHAPTER 8 70
ESTATE TAXES
CHAPTER 9 77
LETS TALK ABOUT TAX CREDITS
SPECIAL OFFER FOR YOU 79
ABOUT THE AUTHOR 80
NAVI J. DOWTY, CFA ©
APPENDIX 82

FOREWORD

By Navi Dowty, CFA

With a book like this, there is always a tradeoff. Do you write it technically, so it is mathematically correct for the academics? Or do you make it more general and more accessible to the general public? I have chosen to make this a more general and descriptive book, with some ideas, a minimum of graphs and equations. As I go through the many edits, which I understand may drive the reader crazy. As it also drove me crazy, but some people will use this to reference different ideas, by simply looking in the table of contents and going to a particular section. The great theme of this book is to try to protect yourself from rising taxes. I find myself saying, "If David Walker was right and tax rates double," in many places. I have to repeat this because if you just look at one section, I can't assume that you read the other section about rising taxes. It will affect everything; so, please bear with the repetition.

I watched my grandparents go from being very prosperous when they retired to virtual destitution in their later years. They followed all of the rules that people were told… Work hard. Save your money. They did that! My grandfather was the chief engineer at a paper company. He was pretty much an electrical genius. He built the big power generators and paper machines.

He could build and fix anything. But after he retired, inflation started, and when he died, my grandmother lived on the ever-diminishing purchasing power of her fixed income. They had not counted on that problem. Why would they? For all their lives the job of the Federal Reserve was to protect the value of the dollar. That all changed, and they weren't equipped to change with it.

When I was on a trip at age 12, visiting my grandparents in Los Angeles, I was robbed at knifepoint in the science museum.

These two events formed the basis of my thinking and approach to taking care of my clients. I vowed never to let them be a victim.

The main focus of this book is how to think about your taxes. Also, how to minimize the burden of taxes, so that you can get enough net retirement income to fund your lifestyle in retirement. It looks to me like, for the vast majority of Americans, providing for an adequate income in retirement is by far the most critical strategy needed. I observed long ago that most people approaching retirement do not have a clear vision of how they want their life to look in the future or a plan of how to get there.

If I asked 1,000 people what their plan is, it is basically, "we hope the market keeps going up." A small percentage of Americans have so much money that income is of no concern, but for the vast majority of people approaching retirement, the most vital questions are, "how do I get enough income after taxes and inflation to fund my lifestyle in retirement?"

For most Americans approaching retirement, most of their money is invested in their retirement accounts in the stock market. They are not taking into account the imminent future tax time bomb facing them, and thus are susceptible to one of the biggest financial predators, paying more taxes than they should.

The other thing that eludes most people is the multiple layers of taxation picking away at the average Americans wealth. Remember that Tax Freedom Day is the end of April. That means you have to work for the first four months of the year just to pay all of your taxes.

These are some of the fundamental challenges that need to be addressed, to properly plan to become a Smiling Retiree.

INTRODUCTION

Let's talk about Taxes.

First of all, why bother? Of course, paying taxes is irritating. But of all the things that we could talk about in your financial life, why focus on taxes above all the things that we could direct our attention to? This is because income taxes will probably be your biggest expense in your entire life. If I line up 1,000 people and ask them what their biggest expense is? They will most likely say it's their house. But in most cases, it the income taxes.

> "If you can't explain it simply,
>
> you don't understand it well enough."
>
> Albert Einstein

Introduction

So, if we believe the winningest coach in college basketball, John Wooden, we should control the things that we can actually control. Control the controllable and the fundamentals. And in our financial life, for almost everybody, the biggest controllable is income taxes.

I have run retirement calculations for innumerable individuals, businesses, families, and women on their own, over the last 45 plus years.

And one thing I can tell you for sure is that if you get control of your taxes, your money will usually last 6 to 8 years longer in retirement. Sometimes much longer. So, I dedicate this book to the idea that you are in control of how much income taxes you are going to pay. I will show you a thought process that can help you approach the perfect amount of taxes to pay because it really is in your control. Every line on the tax-form is there because of the life decisions that you have made. What I have found is that most people made those decisions without much regard to the biggest expense that they have, their income taxes. So, let's get started.

Introduction

> "The income tax has made liars out of more Americans than golf."
> --Will Rogers

> "Tax day is the day that ordinary Americans send their money to Washington, D.C., and wealthy Americans send their money to the Cayman Islands."
> --Jimmy Kimmel

> "It's income tax time again, Americans: time to gather those receipts, get out those tax forms, sharpen up that pencil, and stab yourself in the Aorta."
> --D. Barry

CHAPTER 1
HOW TO THINK ABOUT YOUR TAXES

Here's the way to think about the tax law of nearly 75,000 pages.

There are laws, codes, rulings and court cases. The basic rule is that everything is taxable, and nothing is deductible unless there's an exception. The 75,000 pages deal with those exceptions. About a third deals with what is considered to be income and the other two-thirds are concerned with the deductions.

And so, here's the way to think about it. Whenever you see a restriction, it's because the IRS regulations gave you a benefit of a few pages before that. That benefit turned out to be too good, and then they had to restrict it.

A good example is your deductible IRA. You can put money into an IRA and take a deduction of up to $6,000 ($7,000 if you are over the age of 50), as long as you or your spouse have that much or earned more income. But later on, they changed the rules to say, if you also have a retirement plan at work, and you have too much income, which changes every year, you can't have both the IRA deduction, and the 401K deduction.

The same is true with new ROTH IRA contributions. If you have too much income, you can't contribute new money into a ROTH IRA. The IRS giveth and then the IRS taketh away.

The point is that you are in control of this largest expense, your income taxes.

Let me point out what we are talking here, minimizing taxes that you owe. I am not talking about evading taxes. You have to pay the taxes that you owe.

We are not talking about some theory like the ones that you read about promoting the idea that the 13th amendment was never really ratified and so you don't have to pay income taxes.

That could even be true, but I don't recommend testing it. The courts have consistently ruled that you have to pay the taxes that you legally owe.

We are talking about things that are actually in the tax law.

But by strategically planning, maybe we can minimize that amount.

First of all, of course, you need a strategy.

In his famous book, the Art of War, the ancient Chinese general, Sun Tsu, said that "tactics before strategy is the noise before the defeat."

That's pretty good. I think that's also true with all things about finance and most particularly taxes. So, let's come up first with an overall strategy. You have to make a decision right at the beginning.

What do you think the future of taxes will be? Taxes could go up, down, or they could stay the same.

That's pretty obvious. But there is a piece of very good evidence that taxes will probably have to go up, maybe dramatically. You have to decide what you think is going to happen. I can tell you that for most of my time in the investment world of over 45 years, the first 90 percent of it was dedicated to helping people put off paying taxes.

We tried to delay, convert to something else, convert from ordinary income to capital gains, shift the payments due to a future year, almost anything we could legally do to delay paying taxes.

And this was a great strategy because tax rates have steadily come down.

They peaked out the last two years of the Second World War at 94 percent. Right now, the top rate is 37 percent, and it actually got down briefly to 35 percent. The 94 percent rate in the last two years of the Second World War was on $200,000 of taxable income, which was a tremendous amount of money back then.

However, if you go to the seventies, it was still 70 percent, and it was still on only $200,000 of income, so they didn't index it.

They started indexing the rates in the early eighties, and they have been declining ever since.

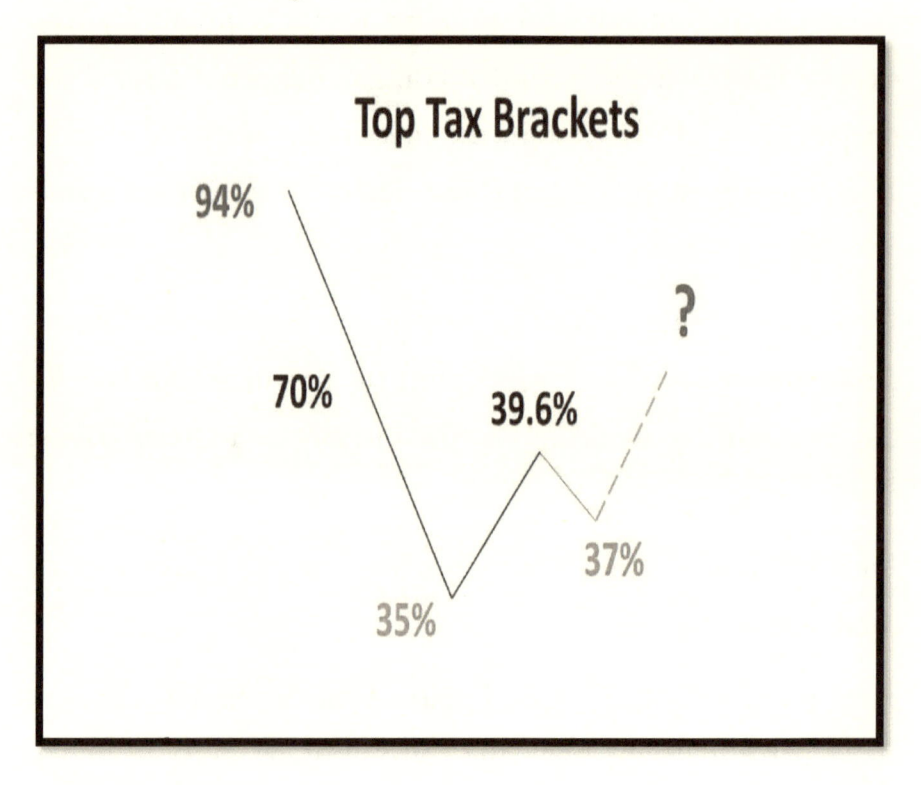

Top Tax Brackets

- 94%
- 70%
- 39.6%
- 35%
- 37%
- ?

Until a couple of years ago. Now they are probably going to rise.

So, what do we think is going to happen? If you ask me what I think, I would say that there are three financial title waves coming.

When do they hit?

I don't know.

And, guess what? Neither does anybody else, although the internet is full of people making predictions.

Interest rates have been going down since October of 1982 when they peaked at 18 percent.

They got down to 2.2 percent in 2017. I think most people would agree that is probably going to be the low point for our lifetime.

In October of 1982, we had 18 percent inflation, at least according to the World Bank. The official rate according to the government was 15 percent.

All three of those major impediments to growth have been coming down, and probably have hit their bottom. So, the question is, what happens next?

> **Why does a slight tax increase cost you two hundred dollars and a substantial tax cut save you thirty cents?**
>
> **A lot of people still have the first dollar they ever made. Uncle Sam has all the others.**

The Crystal Ball

Interest Rates: 5% (1965), 18% (1982), 2.2% (2017)

The Market

Not To Scale and Not A Prediction

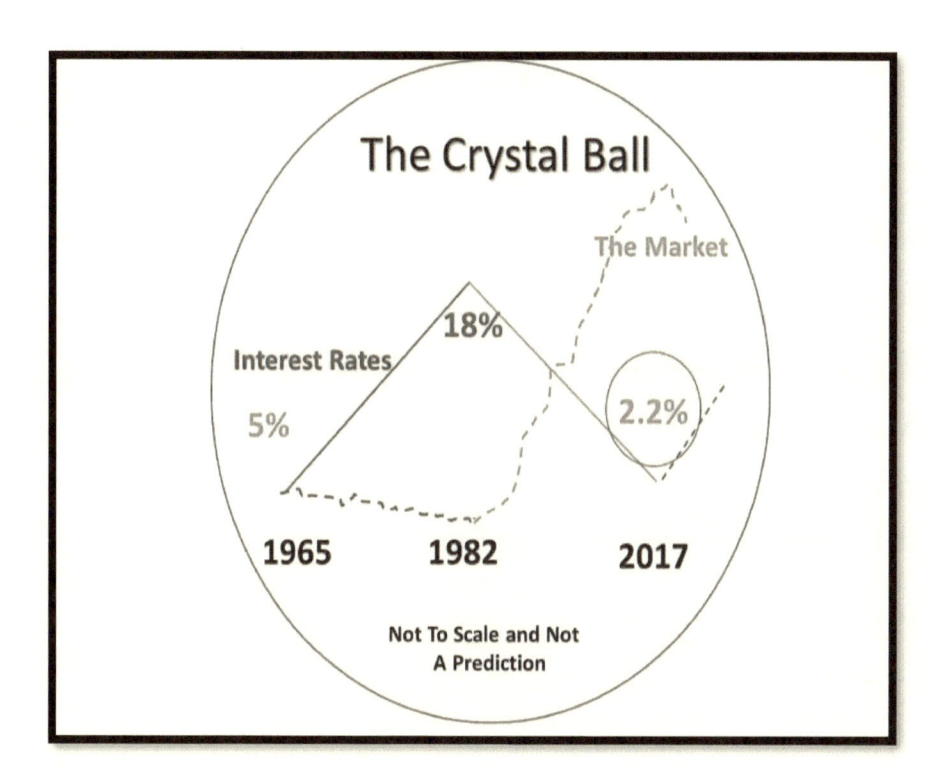

Here is my crystal ball.

If you study this picture, the 2.2% rate that I have circled on the right side is the only number that we can say is probably at an extreme. That extreme probably won't get violated in our lifetime.

I also superimposed a rough sketch of the markets on this graph. This could be a picture of the stock market or the bond market.

That discussion is for another book, but just ponder on what you think has driven the tremendous rise in most financial markets since 1982. You will probably conclude, as I do, that it has been declining interest rates. Tax rates and inflation rates have followed along. Thus the three coming title waves.

There's an informative book, The Power of Zero, by David McKnight and an accompanying documentary movie, which came out in October of 2017. I hosted the world premiere of that movie in Naperville, Illinois.

It's pretty rare that you get to see a documentary in a movie theater, but this is a really good one. If you can see it, I highly recommend it.

In that documentary, numerous people, most prominently David Walker, the former controller general of the federal government, predicted that tax rates would have to double in the future.

I don't know if he's right, but I think it's pretty likely that he is. The average top rate has been 60 percent, and we're at 37 right now, as I write this. Now, of course, you have to add onto that 37 percent, the 3.8 percent investment tax. Some call it the Medicare surcharge tax.

And what about the social security and Medicare tax if you are still working. Those are taxed at 15.3 % of the first about $132,000, for 2019. The number that you are taxed on goes up every year. That is a little over $21,000 of extra tax. Add more if you are a high-income earner, and you have to pay extra Medicare tax. And of course, the Medicare tax doesn't stop at $132,000. You pay the Medicare tax no matter how high your income is.

You might say that you only pay half of that amount and your employer pays the other half. True, but it really comes off of their total cost of having you employed, and of course, if you have your own business, you pay both parts.

And consider this, where will most people get the money to pay the extra social security tax?

By withdrawing more out of their retirement accounts, of course, causing even more tax. And what about the increased tax on that withdrawal amount? They must take more out, and so on and on.

The calculation is that if you must take more out to pay the tax on the tax, and then take more out to pay tax on that, etc. you end up paying about 33% more tax than what you originally thought. And if David Walker was right about the taxes having to go up, that percent will increase even more.

I think it's a pretty good chance that rates will get higher in your retirement years.

We know that rates are going back up on January 1st, 2026 when the current tax law is set to expire. At least, many of the provisions are set to sunset and revert to the 2017 rules.

Most of the changes were actually just suspensions that will disappear in 2026.

So, you have to decide if you think David Walker was right that taxes will be going up a lot in the future.

If so, then you may want to pay more taxes now while taxes are on sale, so to speak.

That's your big overall first strategy decision.

And what do I mean by strategy? President Eisenhower had an overall defense strategy for the United States that was brilliant. If we ever got invaded, we were going to be able to fight a two-front war. That's why we have a US highway system so that he could move troops from the east coast to the west coast and back as needed and land them from troop transport planes on the highway.

Do we work for somebody or start our own business?

Those are big-picture strategies.

So, your first big-picture strategy as it relates to taxes is to decide whether you think rates are going up or down over the foreseeable future, mainly over your retirement years.

> **President Herbert Hoover was the first President to give his salary back to the government.
> Now the government would like everyone to do it.**
>
> **Doing your own income tax return is a lot like a do-it-yourself mugging.**

> "I am proud to be able to pay tax in America, but I could be just as proud paying half the taxes."
>
> --Arthur Godfrey

> "When it comes to taxes, there are two types of people. There are those that get it done early, also known as psychopaths, and then the rest of us."
>
> --Jimmy Kimmel

TAX SECRETS FOR THE SMILING RETIREE

I'm going to assume for the rest of this book that you agree with me that we are somewhere near the bottom in tax rates, and they will probably be going up from here.

And let me clarify something. When I say tax rates, I could just as well say your tax burden. This is because we could have the rates stay the same, but if they eliminate certain deductions, then in effect, you're paying more tax.

So, I can use tax rates or tax burden, interchangeably.

We are talking about you paying more money out of your pocket for income taxes when the tax rates increase. We're talking primarily here of course, about federal income taxes.

So, if we're going to try and figure out how you get the most net income to fund your lifestyle in retirement, which is the main criteria for most people in America, we must look at the biggest expense, and that's the taxes.

> "And there are a lot of new taxes coming. California state legislators want to solve our state's giant deficit by taxing marijuana. Meanwhile, Oregon wants to increase a tax on beer, while New York wants Internet porn. You know what this means? By the end of spring break, this whole thing could be paid for."
>
> --Jay Leno

CHAPTER 2
TAXES ARE MYSTERIOUS

I know that income taxes are a little mysterious for most people.

I can remember when I first started to understand income taxes, how mysterious it all seemed to me. And by that, I don't mean you can't just type the numbers into your tax software and produce your tax return. But really knowing your way around your 1040 form is kind of a big deal.

I used to do the tax returns by hand, of course. I'd go to each line of the tax return, starting at the top, and it would ask for the amount of your W2 income?

I would take your W2 forms from your various employers, and I'd add them all up with a calculator and put the total on the W2 line.

Then I would go to the interest and dividends lines. If you had interest or dividends, I'd take your 1099 forms and put it on the worksheet, fill it out by hand, add them all up and then transfer that number over to the 1040 form.

And if you think about it, that's all the 1040 form really is. It is a collection place where all these sub-forms add up all the numbers.

It's much more efficient now that computers do most of the work, but I think most people have lost the sense of knowing their way around the form, and where all the numbers are generated.

It's kind of like, how we used to read maps, and knew our way around? Now, most people just get turn by turn directions from their navigation software, and we are losing the skill of finding our way around.

Here's a way to think about your taxes. Every line on that 1040 form is there because of some activity that you performed. That's good because that means that if you don't like a line on your 1040 form, you can make different decisions.

I'm not saying, don't put the correct numbers on the form. I'm talking about lifestyle decisions.

You have W2 income because you work for a company that produces the W2 tax reporting form. Or you may be working for yourself and then giving yourself a W2.

However, in either case, it's based on a decision that you made. The same is true with the interest and dividends and so on.

Except for your pension. With your pension, once you turn it on, it is pretty hard to change. In fact, you probably can't change it. Check with your tax strategist before turning on your pension. Carefully consider trying to get your company to let you take your pension money as a rollover, rather than an inflexible pension payment. I have had many people in the last few years, who were told all of their working lives that they did not have the option to take their retirement as a lump sum. They were told that they had to take the monthly income. In several cases, at the last minute, the company changed their mind and gave the people a choice of a lump sum.

Of course, it all depends on the numbers; whether you are better off one way or the other. The basic idea is that if you get the rollover, you are in control. If you get the pension, it is inflexible and irreversible.

You can change most everything else on your tax return. Rather than have taxable interest; you can have tax-deferred interest or tax-free interest. Rather than dividend-paying stocks causing you ever more taxes, you can have non-dividend paying stocks.

After all, there is a good chance that the company can reinvest the money that they would pay out in dividends back into their internal growth. They probably can make more money in the long run than you can make, on an after-tax basis if they pay it out to you in the form of dividends. If that is not true, maybe you should be investing in a different company.

There is always a choice to make on every line of your tax return; at least, before you turn on something like your pension or Social Security.

I can remember the early seventies when I used to travel all over the country in corporate America. I called on the local paper mills as the technical representative for the raw materials supplier that I worked for. I would troubleshoot any issues that occurred with our products. When I was finished at night, I would go to the local book store.

I found myself reading the early real estate investing books, most memorably William Nickerson's fantastic book, "how I turned $1000 into $1,000,000 in real estate, in my spare time."

Nickerson was a Ma Bell employee, and one of the first to popularize do it yourself real estate investing. I ate it up!

Eventually, I made enough money doing my real estate investing, that I quit my corporate job and launched my investing career. I would find buildings that needed upgrading or remodeling.

I remember the first time I did a remodeling job with someone else. I ran across a couple that had a 4-unit apartment. They wanted me to sell it for them.

So, I tried. I advertised it and one of the people who came to see it was a builder, but he just wasn't that hot on the idea of this 4 unit because it really needed a lot of work and it was vacant. But it was in a pretty good location.

And so, I said to the builder, "I'll buy it with you." He said, okay. So we remodeled it, sold it and made a good profit. That was long before the house flipping craze.

And then we thought, well, why not just start developing real estate? We'll build apartment buildings. We started with small duplexes and over time built bigger and bigger buildings. Our customers for the small buildings were people looking to enhance their income. But with the bigger buildings, our advertisements attracted more affluent investors with much higher incomes.

I remember building those buildings. And I would attract high-income people; doctors, dentists, entrepreneurs, and corporate executives.

And I was a pretty good builder.

For instance, I would make two completely separate walls between the apartments. I'd have an empty space, then soundboard, then a two by six wall with fiberglass insulation in it, another layer of soundboard, and then drywall. I separated each unit that way. It was really sound-proofed. No wires or pipes penetrated each wall. You could set a cannon off in one apartment, and you couldn't hear it in the other one. I even had a cutaway model made, showing the intricacies of this sitting on my desk, showing these separated sound walls.

I was very proud of this. And I would show this model to all of my affluent customers. I explained to them how I used three quarter inch marine grade tongue and groove plywood on the floors rather than particle board underlayment. And they'd say, "Oh, that's nice. What about the tax savings?"

So, after doing this several times, I finally realized that saving taxes mattered more to them than the details of the construction.

And back then in the seventies, there were even more tax saving benefits from new construction. At that time, you had to make up your own depreciation schedule. Of course, they used the shortest time they could, so that they got bigger deductions.

In the early eighties, Congress changed the depreciation schedule for residential property to twenty-seven and a half years. That is about a 3.6% deduction per year for the next 27 years. For a brief time in the early eighties, it was 12 years! You could write that whole building off in 12 years!

That was a great tax benefit.

You could prepay next year's interest back then.

If you bought a building by the end of the year, you could get a half year's depreciation deduction.

Invariably over the Christmas holidays, I would take my family over to visit my folks in Michigan. The kids were there playing with their cousins, and I would get a phone call the day after Christmas.

It would go something like this, "Hey, you remember that building you were telling me about? Can I still get a half a year's depreciation? I read in some newspaper that I can get a big tax deduction if I close on it by the end of the year. I've got the money. Can we get it done by December 31?" Of course, I replied yes.

So, I'd rush all the family back in the last couple of days after Christmas. I would have two days to get a whole building deeded over to get them that half year's depreciation write-off. Sometimes they would even prepay the next year's interest also.

So, they got tremendous write-offs, and that was why they did it.

Remember back then, the top rate was still 70 percent, so they were really paying a lot of taxes. Remember the term stagflation in the late 70's? You got pushed into higher tax brackets by inflation, even when your money was not buying more because of the same inflation. Your money bought less, and you paid more taxes. The economy was faltering and in a perpetual recession.

Not that we're not paying a lot of taxes now, but it's a lot less on the same amount of income now than it was way back then.

In the mid-'70s a friend of mine was doing commercial real estate development. I was developing residential buildings, and by that time, I was building some pretty big apartment buildings.

We decided we might as well do it together. So, we formed a corporation.

I can still remember the first time we met with a CPA going over the corporate tax return. I remember how I felt about it. It was like a blur. It had line after line, of all these numbers, and it just all seemed very mysterious and confusing.

And I said to myself, "I have got to learn this. If he can understand it, I can understand it too. This is really important."

So, I started studying taxes and have done that for all the rest of my career.

Since then, I've focused my practice largely around the tax question.

How do we optimize your income and minimize your taxes? That's largely the focus of my unique trademarked process, the **Smiling Retiree Process** ®.
It's about how do we optimize your income and minimize your taxes; so that you can have enough net income to fund your lifestyle in retirement.

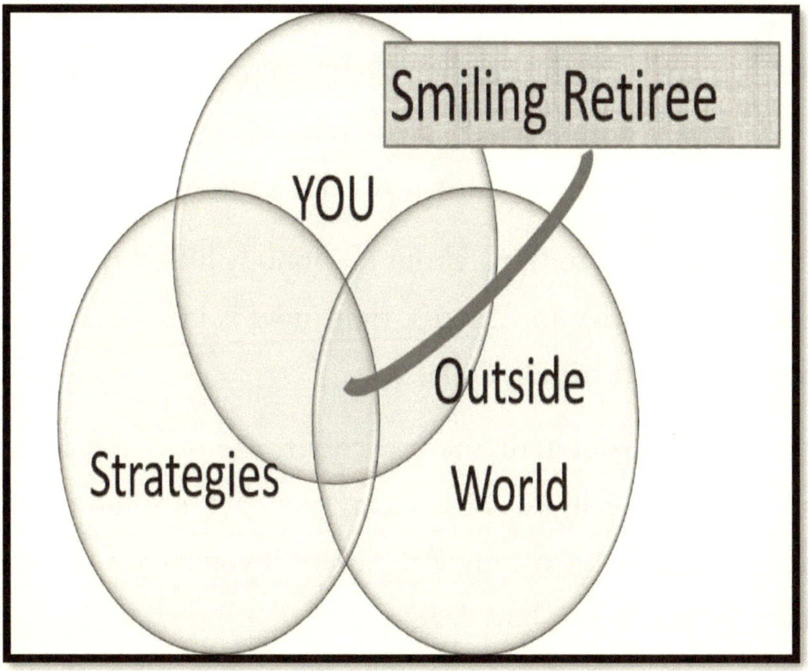
Smiling Retiree
YOU
Outside
World
Strategies

CHAPTER 3
TAXES ARE ON SALE

So that's the backstory.

What about now? If you believe that taxes are going to go up in the future, then what you're really saying is that taxes are on sale. If so, then we may want to subject some of your income to more taxes. That sounds like heresy.

But here's the way to think about it. Nobody likes paying taxes. Most of the money in America right now is in retirement accounts, about 24 trillion dollars.

If you look at your retirement account, the question is, how much of that is really yours? Let's say you have 4 million dollars in your retirement accounts. Add a zero if you have a lot more. Subtract a zero if you have less.

That's not all yours. There's a Lien on it by the IRS. The IRS lent you the tax money, and now you're managing their part of it for them.

That's a pretty good deal for them, and it's actually been a pretty good deal for both you and the IRS. You're taking care of the tax money for the IRS. They like that, but they lent it to you, and for all your life, it's been very smart to do it that way.

So, it's not your fault that you have this gigantic tax bill coming due.

You have been incentives to do that. This is because the rates have steadily declined, and you got a deduction at a high rate, and you plan to repay at a low rate. That is a great arbitrage.

Let's say that you put money in a retirement account when the top rate was 50 percent and now it's 37 percent, so you saved money at 50 percent and now you have to pay it back at 37 percent or even lower if you have less income now. That's pretty smart.

But now rates are set to go back up rather than continuing to go down.

CHAPTER 4
THE QUESTION IS WHAT HAPPENS NEXT?

We think rates are going up. If that's true, then we may want a subject some of our money to the lower rates that we have right now while taxes are on sale. They go back up on January first, 2026 if Congress does nothing.

Most of the new tax law was merely a suspension of the current law, and there are endless examples of that.

For instance, they've doubled the estate tax exemption from five to 10 million indexed for inflation. That goes back to 5 million, adjusted for inflation of course in 2026.

The single and married filing jointly brackets are lower and exactly double each other. That is a slight simplification. All those go back by January first, 2026.

On top of that, of course, is the fact that 78 million baby boomers are retiring at a breakneck rate. They all reach retirement age for social security purposes between 2013 and 2031.

What happens when they retire?

They stop putting new money into social security and Medicare. Their employer stops putting an equal amount as well.

They also stop putting new money into the market as well. Their employer stops matching their funds and is no longer putting new money into the market for them into their retirement plans. At least, when I asked my classes that question, you might be surprised to know that nobody raised their hands to claim their former employer is still adding money to their 401K.

So, what do you do? Maybe pay some of your taxes while they are on sale.

We all like bargains. And, if taxes are going to go up, they are probably a bargain right now.

It is like going to garage sales in the winter.

There is always something you can do to save taxes, and it is like prospecting for gold on your tax return!

CHAPTER 5
SAVING TAXES RIGHT NOW

Before we get to that, however, let's look at some of the ways that we might save taxes right now.

Let's take a brief interlude and talk about different ways to reduce your current taxes.

After all, you still might want to reduce your taxes temporarily, if you're in the top two tax brackets.

We can always deal with how to get the money out of your various retirement accounts later on.

For instance, the IRS just raised the maximum deduction, for you funding your retirement accounts to $333,000. That of course, will change every year.

You might say, wait a minute. I thought the amount that I could contribute to my IRA was $6,000, or $55,000 into my self-employed SEP IRA, or $25,000 into my 401k at work, or $55,000 into my solo 401k.

That's all true but remember this idea. There is always a way if your tax strategist is creative enough.

For instance, if you have your own company, and you're older, and your employees are younger, you can have what's known as a defined benefit retirement plan. They just raised that maximum rate for all the combined deductions going to you by putting all forms of retirement plan deductions together, to $333,000.

Obviously, everybody won't get that much, and it requires some calculations, but a good tax planner can do that for you.

So, here is the key message in this book, get together with your tax planner immediately, not tomorrow, not next week, and not next month. Do it now, because a lot of the things that we are going to talk about are time sensitive. If you do them on January second, you'll have much better results than if you do them on June 30th or December 15th. So, get together with your tax planner today as you're reading this book.

One way to reduce the immediate tax bill is to put the money into a qualified retirement plan, and you can do that at work. Of course, if you have your own business, you can set up your own retirement plans. I alluded to that, and you can deduct up to $55,000 for a 401K. You have to include your employees of course, and if you do a defined benefit plan, you can deduct up to up to $333,000.

You can do that for yourself in your own IRA up to $6,000 for both husband and wife, or if you're over 50, each can have up to $7,000 into a deductible IRA.

However, those numbers start to phase out at $103,000, if you have a retirement plan at work. You're no longer able to do the deductible IRA at all after you hit $123,000 of income.

So, the best thing, of course, is to have your own business and then you're in control of all that.

However, lots of people who read this book will be employees, and they don't have that control.

So, one of the questions is, should you maximize your retirement account deduction at work?

Like everything else in this book, it requires a calculation. If you just look online for help, you will get rules of thumb, but your situation truly is unique, and your calculations and strategy should be unique as well.

Your tax planner can help you figure out what of the many strategies best optimize your present and future wealth.

What other actions can we take to reduce your current taxes?

How about if you have a small business and you have children?

Could you have them working in your business?

I was thinking about this as I was sitting in the conference room at my property management company last summer. The guy who runs the property management company had his kids out from raking the lawn.

I asked him, "do you pay them for working?" He said, "No, they work. I just don't pay them." I told him that maybe he should be paying them. After all, they are working.

I mean, it must be legitimate, but they're working.

And the first $12,200 of earnings per person isn't even taxable under the new tax law.

So, think of this. Let's say there is a husband and wife with three kids. That's five people multiplied by $12,200. If the kids really do work in the business, the family could have up to the first $61,000 for their family, which is not even taxable because that's the standard deduction now for every person. And the next approximately $79,000 is only taxed at 10% to 12%. That's probably as low as it's going to get for the rest of your life. So, that's an idea.

Here's another idea.

How about taking part of that income that you pay the kids and put it into a Roth IRA for them. That would be way better than a 529 plan. And what you've just done is made a Roth

IRA tax deductible and it's tax-free for them for the rest of their lives.

You know, you're buying stuff for them anyway. You can figure out what to do with their money after they earn it. You are in charge as the custodian. You are probably saving up money for their college anyway; so, why not pay them? You get a deduction and teach them about working, and money management, and saving plans.

How about this idea?

Seventy-eight million baby boomers are charging into retirement.

That's one of the big reasons David Walker says taxes have to go up. He pointed out that social security is out of money in 2034 and Medicare is out of money in 2026, and social security and Medicare is already 40 percent of the federal budget. These statistics are from the Board of Trustees for Social Security and Medicare.

The Social Security Board of Trustees figures that they will be able to pay about 77% of the currently scheduled benefits after 2034 through tax revenues until about 2080.

There are seventy-eight million baby boomers and many of them have parents who are paying down their fortune for medical expenses and long-term care.

Many of those parents don't have enough income to be able to deduct medical expenses. What happens to those lost deductions?

Are they carried forward? Nope! What if they die. Do their heirs get to take them? Nope!

They just lose the deductions. They are gone forever!

That is billions and billions and billions of dollars of lost deductions.

Suppose that you get those medical expenses as deductions on your tax return as their child?

Can you do that?

Yes, under the right conditions.

You have to jump thru some hoops, but it might be worth it if you could put a big dent in your tax bill. Any good tax planner can show you how to do that.

It depends on your own specific set of circumstances of course, but get together with your tax planner right away, and they can show you how to get that deduction.

It is time sensitive though, because every month that goes by, you lose 1/12 of the deduction.

I've seen this technique will be able to wipe out a couple's tax bill entirely.

Imagine a husband and wife, each paying $100,000 a year for medical expenses and long-term care. They're in a nursing home or a medical facility, and they have normal pensions and social security, but nowhere near enough to use up all those deductions.

What happens if they end up with a $150,000 negative taxable income?

They just lose it.

So, why waste billions and billions of dollars on the deductions that are not being used every year by people, just for not taking advantage of the deductions that are right there? It doesn't hurt your parents at all.

Even if you have to jump through some hoops to properly set this up to take the deductions, why not do it? Like I said, any good tax planner can show you how to do that. If they can't use the deductions, why waste them?

And while we are talking about your parents, maybe it would pay to talk to them about converting some of their retirement accounts into ROTH IRAs.

I know it might be an uncomfortable conversation for many people, but if you inherit an IRA or another retirement account, you cannot convert it yourself. It is a

prohibited transaction for tax purposes. Only your parents can make that election on their retirement accounts. In many cases, the children are in their highest tax brackets, while the parents are at their lowest.

Once the children inherit the retirement accounts, they have to begin taking taxable withdrawals out. If your parents convert them to ROTHS, and you inherit the accounts, you still have to take out withdrawals, but they are not taxable. Do you understand that?

And remember, ROTH IRA withdrawals do not cause any tax on your social security benefits. It might even pay you to pay the tax on the conversion for your parents. Of course, this only applies if your parents are in lower tax brackets, but it is worth considering.

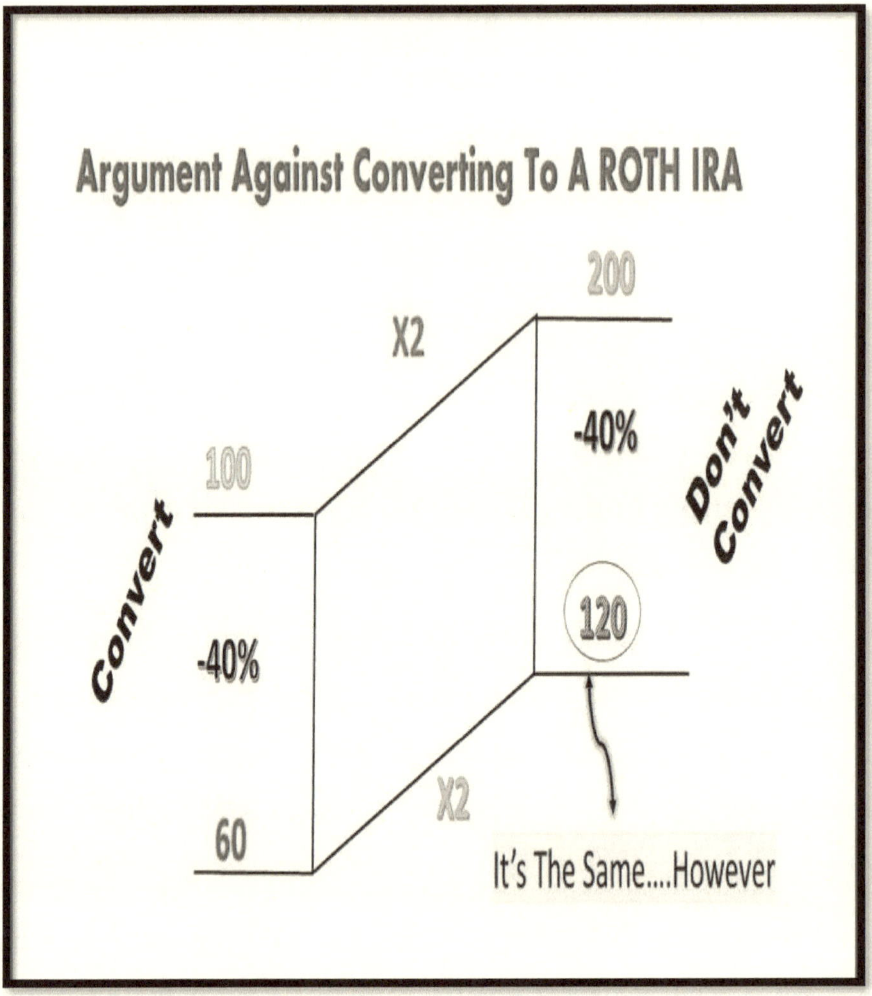
Argument Against Converting To A ROTH IRA
200
X2
-40%
Don't Convert
100
Convert
-40%
120
X2
60
It's The Same....However

Here is a picture showing what some people talk about as an argument against converting to a ROTH.

The idea is that if you convert now and pay the taxes, or if you convert at some time in the future and pay the taxes then, you end up with the same amount. In the case of this illustration, 120.

However, that is only true if we ignore four things.

1) Tax rates may go up
2) Taking out a larger amount in the future may push you into a higher tax bracket. It might cause even more tax on your retirement account withdrawals.
3) The larger amount in the future may cause more tax on your social security
4) When your heirs inherit what is left, they may be in a higher tax bracket, and they are not allowed to convert an inherited IRA.

So, if you convert now, it should be insulated from future tax problems.

Another question, of course, is what if the government changes the law and decides to tax ROTHS IRA'S or other tax-free sources of income in the future?

That would be a pretty big and dramatic change.

Many members of Congress, senators, fortune 500 companies and other affluent people who have used these strategies would vigorously oppose this change because they use these same strategies.

Also, wouldn't it be much easier just to raise the rates on the existing retirement accounts? After all, that is where all the money is. Why precipitate a constitutional crisis to tax only 3% of the retirement money? It is reported that 3% is how much is in ROTHs as I write this. It might be much easier to go after the big pot of money in 401K's and IRA's and leave alone the tiny amount that has already been taxed. There is also the idea that usually changes are grandfathered under the old rules.

What else?

There are some more aggressive strategies that you might use.

You could get tax deductions for real estate. A strategy you might use is to finance the real estate enough so that it just breaks even. Then, you take the depreciation as a negative deduction on your tax return. It comes off on line 17 as a minus.

Since the early eighties, the tax rule has been that the maximum you can take for those real estate deductions against your active income is $25,000 a year if you actively participate in the real estate.

The problem, of course, is that when you hit the fourth tax bracket, the phaseout starts and you don't get the deductions in the current year. Those deductions, however, are suspended, and you get them back when you sell the building, as long as you are alive.

However, that's not much comfort right now when you thought you were going to get a deduction for the real estate.

And those suspended deductions die with you, so don't waste them.

Other investment activities that can give you current year deductions are things like oil, gas and solar. You'd get somewhere around 85 percent deduction on oil and gas drilling.

You can get about a 40 percent write-off for solar farm investments.

If you own part of these oil and gas operations or solar energy farms, can also get ongoing income, if they make money.

You can also just contribute highly appreciated property, like real estate or securities to charity. You could just give those to a charity outright and then get the deduction, or you can give them to a charity and get an income.

Probably a better way for most people is to set up your own charitable trust. You give the property to the charity, your charitable trust.

You take the deduction this year. But more importantly, when you sell the property, there's no tax to pay. And then you get income for life out of the charitable trust.

That's a pretty good strategy.

You do get to take the deductions, and there are many forms of that charitable trust.

You could give the income; you could give the future value or the present value.

You could loan the charity the property and give them the income, get it back in the future, and get a big current deduction to offset a high-income year.

There are innumerable different versions that can be designed, each tailor-made for you.

These can all be structured to give you the tax effect that you need, at the same time helping your favorite charity and leaving your legacy, while getting living benefits of current income and deductions now. Any good tax planner should be able to help you design a program based on your current needs.

That's another way to do it.

And finally, in the charitable realm, there's an even more aggressive strategy, and that's a Charitable Land Trust.

The IRS doesn't like this kind of Charitable Land Trusts very much because there have been abuses in the past.

So, tread carefully here.

Make sure that you're not dealing with one that would be considered to be abusive and you have to be an accredited investor even to have anybody talk to you about this kind of investment. I am telling you about it as an educational idea. You need to be dealing with someone who knows this area if you are contemplating using this strategy. Just know that they exist and that it's a possibility that you can frequently get multiples of what you contribute as a deduction.

Again, any good tax planner can show you how to do that.

Let's talk about your house as a tax deduction. What can you do with your house? You can rent your house to your company. If you rent your house to your company for your annual meeting, there is a De minim-is 14 days per year that you can rent out your house and not pay tax on the proceeds. Can you have your office in your house and conduct business in your office, as part of your house and get a tax deduction? Yes, of course.

Anything that a big company does, your company can do. So, look at what the big companies do.

I remember walking out of the bank one day and saw their annual report setting on the desk by the door. I noticed on the back that it said the bank was owned by a holding company of the same name, headquartered in Las Vegas!

Why would a local bank Holding Company be headquartered in Las Vegas?

Well, for one thing, they saved income taxes. But also, they had their annual meeting in Las Vegas.

It turns out the guys on the board like to go to shows, gamble at the casinos, and that's where they had their annual meeting.

If they can do it, you can also do it.

Can you have your annual meeting on a cruise ship? No!

Pretty clearly you can't do that.

How about Hawaii? No!

However, you can have it in the North American territory. What's the North American territory? Well, it covers the Caribbean Islands and all of continental North America.

It's pretty clear that you can't have your company's annual meeting on a cruise ship.

However, could you use the cruise ship as transportation to get there? And of course, the answer is yes, up to certain limits.

We should also talk about tax-free exchanges.

The code allows you to exchange certain things for other things without paying current taxes on the gains. The most common of those things is Real estate held for investment purposes, or trade or business.

What that means is that if you have a candy store, and your business has expanded, and you want to trade your small store in and get a bigger store, you don't have to pay tax on the gain of the small store. It just makes sense, and that is the law.

It also applies to investment real estate. Of course, there are rules that must be followed.

At my office or one of my classes, people frequently ask, "we just sold our apartments, how can we save taxes on the gain?"

Unfortunately, it is too late for these tax-free exchanges. The tax-free exchanges are off the table once the sale is closed. We have to use other repair strategies. This must be set up before the sale is finalized. See your tax planner long before you start trying to sell your real estate.

These are frequently called 1031 exchanges referring to the code section 1031 that allows tax-free exchanges of this type.

Your house is an exception. The rules for the sale of your house are that every two years, you can exclude $250,000 from gain per person. So, husband and wife can exclude $500,000 of gain every two years from the sale of their primary residence. Most of us won't hit those lofty numbers every two years.

Before the new tax law, equipment was included in the exchange rules. So, a farmer would trade in a tractor at the end of the year for a new shiny one. He probably expensed the whole value of the tractor the year that he bought it, so his tax cost basis is zero.

When he traded it, his tax cost basis carried over to the new tractor, and he didn't have to pay the income tax or sales tax, on the old tractor's value. The new tax law eliminated the ability to trade in equipment under section 1031 of the code. So, disposing of old equipment is going to come as a surprise for many businesses when they get taxed on the trade in value of tractors, trucks, forklifts, etc. because they will produce taxable gains.

> Death and taxes are inevitable, but death doesn't repeat itself.
>
> The wealth of experience is one possession that hasn't been taxed . . . yet.
>
> Golf is a lot like taxes. You drive hard to get to the green and then wind up in the hole.

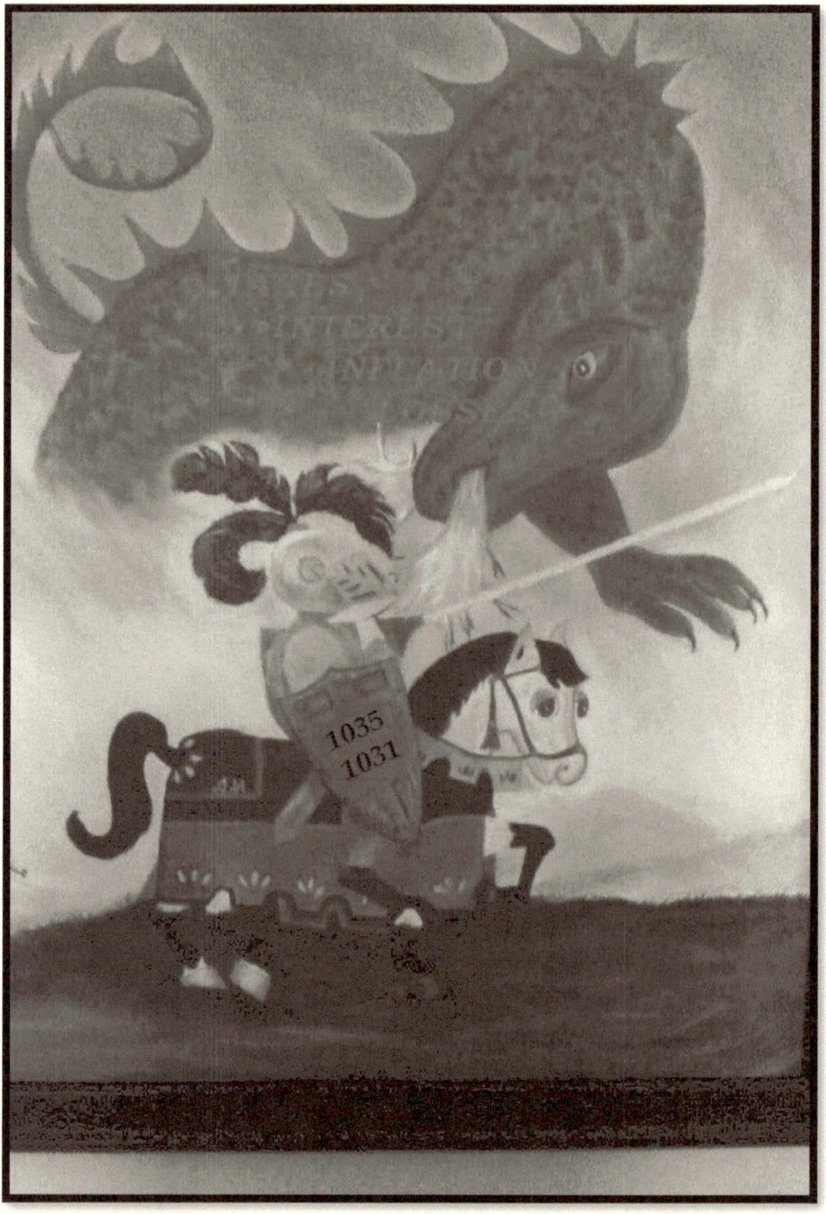
1035
1031

Another part of tax-free exchanges is retirement account to retirement account rollovers, life insurance to life insurance and, annuity to annuity contracts. These are covered under section 1035 and are frequently referred to as 1035 exchanges.

Those are some of the more common deductions that you can use to reduce current income tax. Of course, there are many more. More than we could ever cover in this short book. These are just to get you thinking about your taxes.

If you're in the top two tax brackets and depending on how much you have in your retirement accounts already, you may still want to maximize your deductions because it will reduce your taxes in the current year.

What other ways can you use to save current taxes?

Well, charitable itemized deductions are a big thing.

You still have the deduction for charitable contributions.

In fact, they even raised the charitable deduction to be 60 percent of your adjusted gross income for cash contributions up from 50 percent.

This new tax law, of course, reduced the amount of deductions you can have for state and local taxes to $10,000. This limitation is not a big deal for people that live in rural areas and don't have a lot of property taxes.

However, if you live in New York, Chicago, San Francisco, or other high property tax areas, this is going to be a very, very big hit. I've looked at many tax returns last year where the people had $65,000, $75,000, $85,000, $110,000 or more in itemized deductions and they're not going to be able to itemize anymore at all. This loss of deductions will be a very big tax hit to them.

> "Blessed are the young, for they shall inherit the national debt."
>
> --Herbert Hoover

Let's summarize the things that we've lost. We lost a lot of deductions from state and local property taxes. Like I say, down to $10,000.

You still have medical deductions. Anything above seven and a half percent of your adjusted gross income can be a deduction.

You can still have interest deductions on your primary residence and a second house. The loans have to be secured on those houses separately, and they can't exceed a million dollars if you want to deduct the interest.

Can you borrow money on your principal residence to buy the second home and deduct the interest?

Not, anymore.

We also lost all the miscellaneous itemized deductions, such as tax prep fees, investment management fees, unreimbursed employee business expenses, moving expense deductions, and casualty losses. You can't deduct casualty losses unless they are from a federally designated disaster area.

Employees like teachers that spend a lot of money buying things for their jobs, and employees that drive their personal cars to work will not get to deduct those expenses anymore.

Here's another change.

For a while back in the seventies and early eighties, you could put properties in your children's name and take advantage of the fact that the kids were not in a high tax bracket.

Then Congress got wise to that ploy and started taxing minor children's passive income at the parent's tax rate.

The new tax law does away with that. Now the rule is simplified. You no longer have to tax the kids at the parent's tax rate. The kids will be taxed at the trust rates.

The highest rates.

If their passive income gets above $12,000, then we're talking about the maximum rate, which is 37 percent. So, simplification does not always equal savings.

If we're not talking about too much income, it's still possible to benefit. If you are only talking about a few thousand dollars, you can still shift some to the kids and possibly benefit. It's a calculation just like everything else in this book.

> **The hardest thing in the world to understand is Income tax**
>
> --Albert Einstein

Entertainment is out as a deduction.

Losing entertainment deduction will be a very big deal for many businesses.

So, if you have your own business and you used to take clients to a golf outing, that's no longer available to deduct for small businesses and corporations alike.

What was not taken away is the deduction for gifts.

So, rather than taking somebody golfing, you may want to give them a ticket for green fees, because gifts are still able to be deducted if they are appropriate, necessary, and customary for your business.

> About the time a man is cured of swearing, another income tax is due.
>
> Come to think of it, these income-tax forms leave little to the imagination and even less to the taxpayer.
>
> It is difficult to predict the future of an economy in which it takes more brains to figure out the tax on our income than it does to earn it.

CHAPTER 6
HOW ABOUT BUSINESSES

The new big benefit for businesses is a reduction in taxes.

So, if you're operating your business as a C Corporation, they lowered the maximum tax rate from 37 percent to 21 percent.

That's a pretty big reduction.

What about all the other businesses?

Most businesses in America are small businesses. Most small businesses in America are sole proprietorships. The sole proprietorship also gets a tax savings; although, it's a little funky.

The sole proprietor's tax saving comes off as a deduction on his personal tax return.

What am I talking about? Most small businesses file their business taxes on their schedule C on the front side of their personal 1040 tax form.

Whatever the net income from that business is, it is reduced by a 20 percent deduction on line 9 of the tax return just above their taxable income line.

The same is true if you operate as an S Corp or an LLC.

However, this deduction doesn't show up at all on your company tax return.

Income from your own business shows up on the front side of your tax return, and it will either show up on your schedule C, or if it's an S Corp or an LLC, it'll show up on line 4b. These are called pass-through entities.

But then, just above your taxable income on line10 of your return, you'll get to take off 20 percent if your total income is under the 5th tax bracket, which in 2019 is $321,451.

It is indexed for inflation, so when you read this, the number may be different, but the concept is the same.

If your income is above $321,400, it phases out over the next hundred thousand dollars.

And when your personal income hits $421,400, you don't get any deduction at all for your small business.

Unless your business is architecture or engineering. Why architecture and engineering? I guess they just liked architects and engineers.

This is a pretty big anomaly because you could have two people that own a business. One of them gets the 20 percent reduction, and the other one who has too much income doesn't get the 20 percent reduction.

Because the 20 percent deduction occurs after the calculation of your adjusted gross income, the business income still affects taxation on your social security distributions.

So, let's talk about that for a second.

You may wonder, are my social security benefits going to be taxed if I'm taking social security and I'm still running your business?

Social Security is tax-free up to a provisional income of $32,000 for a couple, at which time 50 percent of it has been taxed.

And then at $44,000, 85 percent of it starts to get taxed.

The thresholds are $25,000 and $34,000 for single taxpayers.

That provisional income is determined by taking half of your social security payments, and then adding to that, your modified adjusted gross income. Modified meaning that you take the bottom number on the front side of your tax form, and add back any tax-free municipal bond interest, and deductions you had such as IRA'S.

> **Worried about an IRS audit? Avoid what's called a red flag. That's something the IRS always looks for. For example, say you have some money left in your bank account after paying taxes. That's a red flag.**
>
> --Jay Leno

The effect of all that is you don't get the deduction for what's called the QBI, qualified business income to reduce taxes on your social security. That deduction comes off after the calculation of your social security tax.

So, to make the long story short, we won some, and we lost some.

And where you end-up really depends on your characteristic, income, and deductions that occur on each line of the tax return.

As I have said, each one of those lines is a choice that you've made. And if you've made a choice, you can unmake that choice and change it for the future if it benefits you.

CHAPTER 7
PAY TAXES NOW

Let's now go back to the original premise of this book.

If taxes are really likely to increase, possibly dramatically in the future, then we have a golden opportunity to take advantage of the sale going on right now. Maybe we want to pay some of the taxes now.

This is because rates are pretty low right now compared to the past, and probably the future as well.

The first two brackets are 10 and 20 percent.

That's probably as low as it's ever going to be in your lifetime.

So, what will happen if we say we're going to shift money from the taxable area or the tax-deferred retirement account area over to the tax-free or tax-advantaged area, how would that work?

Well, the most obvious is a Roth conversion.

You can convert the money from a regular retirement account to a ROTH 401K or a ROTH IRA.

You can also put new money into a ROTH, and you can do that every year up to $6,000 if you have at least $6000 of income. Your spouse can also contribute the same amount, and if you're over 50, you can both contribute $7,000.

Now, of course, that's limited. If your income is too high, you can no longer contribute to a new ROTH.

However, you can convert to a ROTH irrespective of your income size.

Can you contribute to a nondeductible IRA and then immediately convert to the so-called back door ROTH? The answer is yes.

Converting a non-deductible IRA to a ROTH IRA was discussed at the conference meetings between the House and the Senate five times in the new tax law conference. It survived and stayed in the new law. So, you are still able to make a non-deductible IRA contribution and then convert it to a ROTH.

As I have said before, any good tax planner can help you with this.

Let's say you will like to have some more deductions for last year.

Can you make an IRA contribution, assuming that your income is under $103,000 or you don't have a retirement plan at work, and take the deduction for last year and then immediately convert it to a ROTH IRA for the current year?

Absolutely, it will be taxable in the next year rather than last year. Assuming, of course, that you do this before April 15.

So, what else can we do?

Suppose that you didn't have the cash available right now. It's the last minute, and you see that you would like the deduction for last year.

Can you borrow the $7,000 from someone; the bank, a friend, or your family

For just one day? Put the money into the IRA, get the deduction for last year. Take it out the next day and pay it back — one day's interest.

I am not recommending this, just passing it on as a strategy, if you need it; maybe you borrow the money from an account that you have set aside for a future purchase. Of course, it will add to your taxable income this year, but whether it is a good idea is just a calculation, like everything else in this book.

It is all a tradeoff. You always have to give something up, to get something else.

So, let's get back to paying the tax while it is on sale.

You can just pay the tax.

Here are some tactics. Here are some things you can do right now.

A Roth IRA conversion.

If you can convert your money in your 401K, to a ROTH, depends on the plan document that your company has.

An easy thing to do right now is to call your HR department and ask them if they have a way to convert your existing 401k to a ROTH 401K.

You can do the same thing for a 403B plan if you work for a non-profit organization of any kind or the government.

If you cannot convert your retirement account where you're working, then ask them this question, "Can I do a non-hardship, in-service withdrawal?" If the answer to that is yes; then, you can take the money out and send it over to your own IRA and then convert all or part of that to a ROTH.

In fact, you should ask your HR department that question anyway, so that you know all of your options.

That brings up the question, of course, should we do this all at once?

Should you convert everything in your retirement account, all at once?

I think a better strategy is to convert it fast enough so that the conversion is complete by January first, 2026 when rates go back up, but slow enough, so you don't get drawn into a higher tax bracket.

There's a big jump between the second bracket and the third bracket.

And then another big jump between the fourth and fifth bracket, so you'd like to stay in the first two brackets if possible.

You can probably get into the first two brackets or perhaps even into the zero bracket in retirement unless you have a pension with no options,

If you're in the third bracket, you have quite a way to go before you get into the next big jump.

By the way, I am purposely not using numbers here, since they change every year. Just look at the tax tables online.

Could we have done anything else?

Certain forms of life insurance will allow you to get tax free income if they are structured just right.

And from my perspective, the numbers have to work out that. You don't want to just go to the local life insurance salesperson and do this, but under the right circumstances, a cash value life insurance program could be very beneficial and can provide a lifetime of income.

These programs have to be structured just right, or I wouldn't recommend put ting too much into these programs.

If you want to do something like that, here's how I would look at it.

I think of life insurance on a spectrum.

On the far-right side is the term insurance. It will be the least expensive way to buy death benefit if that is what you need.

Let's say you have a young family and you'd like to protect them, and you're 25 years old. You have three kids and a spouse, and you're the breadwinner. If you get hit by a truck, it's really bad for the family.

So, how do we protect them? We protect them by insuring your life so that they can survive if you aren't there to provide for them. We want them to be able to get educated and become productive citizens.

Term life insurance does that.

And it is pretty inexpensive, at least in the beginning.

Of course, the problems with term insurance are that it doesn't provide any income. And it gets really expensive as you get older, so it's almost always canceled at some point.

This isn't so bad because other forms of insurance like our fire insurance isn't likely to pay off either. At least, we hope not.

We aren't that upset when the year goes by, and we didn't have to invoke our fire insurance on our house.

At the other extreme, on the left side, we have single payment insurance.

It's really just an account with the insurance company with insurance attached to it.

You may have money sitting in the bank, and not earning much interest.

Let's say you put in a one-time payment of $100,000. Add some zero's if you have a lot more.

What will you get?

You may have a $200,000 tax-free death benefit, depending on your age and health. You may be able to earn between 0 and 8 percent every year indexed to some market index. The amount you can get credited depends on the economy and the interest rates.

If interest rates go up, you can just use the fixed interest rate.

You may be able to access the death benefit to use as long-term care or even home health care.

You may even get a money back guarantee.

How about tax-free income? The tax rule is that if you put the money in all at once, it is taxable when you take a withdrawal. In other words, they tax the earnings first.

Somewhere in between those two extremes is a line. If you cross over that line, then the taxation of the withdrawal's changes. It is not subject to tax if you take it out as a loan.

What if you take the same $100,000 and put it in over time, say ten years?

Then, if it is structured just right, the withdrawals that you make are not considered to be taxable income.

You may still have long term and home health care benefits and probably a larger tax-free death benefit. You may get to earn anywhere between 0 and 13 percent. These change with the economy.

If you work out the numbers, and your health rating is good, and it is structured just right, this alternative could actually work out better than a ROTH for some of your assets.

My personal rule of thumb is to shift not more than 2-4 percent of your pot of money every year to this strategy.

In between those two extremes falls the art of designing what would be just right for you.

According to Ed Slot, a prominent CPA and author of many bestselling retirement IRA books, the only true tax-free accounts under the code are cash value life insurance and the Roth IRA. Everything else has some form of tax issue.

Tax-free bonds for instance. They are federally tax-free, but only state tax-free in the state where they are issued. And they are subject to capital gains tax if you sell them at a gain or if the mutual fund that holds them for you, sells them at a taxable gain.

Worst of all though, the income from tax-free municipal bonds potentially causes tax on your social security, since it is added back into the calculation for provisional income.

So, they are not really tax-free.

Withdraws from your Roth IRA and from properly structured cash value life insurance is not taxable.

What else can we do?

We can just redirect our 401K contributions at work to our ROTH 401k, so that we will get tax free income in the future when we make withdrawals.

If your work doesn't have that option, most do now, but if yours doesn't, you can direct them to your own ROTH, or your cash value life insurance. If the numbers work out right for you, that's another way to do it.

I can tell you this, if you do all this and get most of your money into the tax-free bracket; you will have many streams of tax-free income.

Let's think of what they might be. What could they be?

They could be things such as withdrawal from your ROTH IRA, and from your ROTH 401K or 403B. You can have withdrawals from your ROTH conversion. You can have withdrawals from properly structured life insurance plans.

If all of these streams of income are tax-free to you, your social security income will probably be tax-free as well.

And finally, each of you can leave some money in your retirement accounts, so that when you take the withdrawals, you are just using your standard deduction. So, those withdrawals will be tax-free as well.

That is twelve different sources of tax-free income for husband and wife. Six if you are single. Then when they raise the tax rates you should be pretty well insulated.

A man's home is his castle. At least that's how he feels when he pays taxes on it.

It's too bad for the middle-income person. They earn too much to avoid paying taxes and make too little to afford paying them.

The average man now lives thirty-one years longer than he did in 1850. He has to, in order to get his taxes paid

The best things in life are free - plus tax, of course.

The best things in life are still free, but the tax experts are working overtime on the problem.

A dime is a dollar with all the various taxes deducted.

Being a success today means the government takes away in taxes what you used to dream of earning.

CHAPTER 8
ESTATE TAXES

We should also talk about the estate tax because it's not on anybody's radar screen anymore. Husband and wife, each have over $10,000,000 deduction, adjusted for inflation. In 2019 the number for the deductions is $11,400,000 So, most people aren't even looking at estate planning anymore.

A couple of points on that, however.

For one thing, the estate tax is going back down to five million, adjusted for inflation, in 2026.

If you add everything up, you may still be above that.

Remember to factor in the value of your business.

The IRS will value your business for estate tax purposes.

The rate is 40% on everything above 10 million adjusted for inflation, about 11.5 million for 2019.

Both husband and wife can get that deduction for Federal estate tax purposes.

However, it will be different if you read this in a different year.

There is a lot of talk about wanting to raise the 40% rate. So, watch carefully.

Many states have a state inheritance tax. In most cases, the State Inheritance Tax exemption did not go up along with the federal estate tax exemption.

In Illinois, for instance, for both husband and wife, everything above 4 million dollars is taxable at up to 16 percent.

In other words, the deduction is not portable like the federal estate tax is. Your exemption dies with you. So, it gets to be a bit more of a complex calculation.

How do we minimize the estate tax?

Before 1982, there was an estate tax even between husband and wife. So, a farmer's wife might have to sell the farm when her husband died to pay the estate tax. There is no longer an estate tax between husband and wife.

Another big aspect of estate planning is the fact that your heirs will get a step up in tax basis for some things that they inherit from you. This step up is only for income tax purposes and doesn't apply to everything they inherited.

The step-up applies to capital assets such as real estate and stocks. The taxable gain disappears. What happens if a husband or wife dies? The survivor gets a step up on half. Unless they live in a community property state.

Then they get a complete step on both halves. The gain disappears!

One of the main missing pieces of estate planning is the idea that life insurance proceeds are tax-free.

That statement is true concerning income tax.

But in almost all cases, life insurance proceeds are subject to estate taxes.

If you have any control over the policy, the proceeds are included in your estate for estate tax purposes. That is a big mistake in many estate plans.

So, if you have more than 11 million dollars, and are certain that you are not going to need it for your lifestyle, one of the strategies is to consider getting some of the excesses completely outside of your estate.

If you have excess, why subject it to unnecessary tax?

We can do that in many different ways.

We can put some of your highly appreciated assets into your own private charity and then have the income go to you and your spouse for your lifetime. Then the balance goes to your charity on your passing.

Or we may want to contribute that excess wealth into a charity that keeps going beyond your lifetime. Your heirs can manage it and make decisions every year about where to donate the money. It can be in your name and go on forever. You can get a current tax deduction as well as create a lasting legacy.

What about selling your business and paying tax on the accumulated gain. Is it taxable? Of course.

Where there's a will, there's an Inheritance Tax.

Another difference between death and taxes is that death is frequently painless.

Blessed are the meek for they shall inherit the earth - less 40 percent inheritance tax

A nervous taxpayer was unhappily conversing with the IRS auditor who had come to review his records. At one point the auditor exclaimed, "We feel it is a great privilege to be allowed to live and work in the USA. As a citizen you have an obligation to pay taxes, and we expect you to eagerly pay them with a smile."
"Thank God," returned the taxpayer. "I thought you were going to want cash."

The tax advisor had just read the story of Cinderella to his four-year-old daughter for the first time. The little girl was fascinated by the story, especially the part where the pumpkin turns into a golden coach. Suddenly she piped up, "Daddy, when the pumpkin turned into a golden coach, would that be classed as income or a long-term capital gain?"

Accountant after reading a nursery rhyme to his child, "No, son. It wouldn't be tax deductible when Little Bo Peep loses her sheep. But I like your thinking."

Can you use some of these charitable strategies to avoid paying tax on the sale of your business? Can we take part of the tax savings and replace the value of the business? Perhaps entirely outside of your estate, so that your wealth passes thru the generations. With this strategy, your wealth isn't continually ravaged by tax after tax, after tax.

Can you restructure how you own your business, so that you can build a mote around it, protecting your heirs against the ravages of future wealth predators? And minimizing the tax bite as well? Yes!

Can we contribute your house to a charity on your death and get a current deduction right now? Yes.

Can we take money out of your retirement accounts offset by the charitable deductions? Yes.

Can we arrange for you to have an income right now, and then replace the money that your kids ultimately inherit, even when you spent the money? Sure!

Can we make sure that the money outside your estate is income and estate tax-free? Yes!

You should review your current estate plan. Many of the old plans had language such that on one spouse's death, the "exemption equivalent" had to be put into the Trust.

That so-called bypass trust is irrevocable. The idea was to avoid losing the deceased spouses' exemption for estate taxes. Back then the exemption was $600,000. Now it is over 11 million. Imagine the dismay when a surviving spouse finds that the old estate plan required that the money she planned to live on was all put in an irrevocable trust. Your attorney can easily fix it if that is the case for your old plan.

All of these are things you should discuss with your tax planner because you need to do the planning if you want to get these results.

It is really about the results that you want. Then there are many possible paths to get those results. If you don't do your own planning, the IRS has a plan for you, and it may not be the plan that you want.

> **You really can't beat the game. If you earn anything, it's minus taxes. If you buy anything it's plus taxes.**
>
> **No matter how staggering the taxes, they never fall down.**

CHAPTER 9
LETS TALK ABOUT TAX CREDITS

A tax credit is usually worth 5 to 10 times a deduction.

If you're in the lower two tax brackets, there are quite a few tax credits that you may be able to get.

The IRS will pay you for working. They'll pay you for saving, they'll pay you for having children, they'll pay you for having the kids taken care of, getting educated, they'll pay you for driving an electric car, and they'll pay you for energy conservation on your house.

These are all called tax credits.

Those are some of the tax credits that are available.

But here's a big one. Husband and wife, three kids, a moderate income of $54,884 may be entitled to $6,431 of earned income tax credit in 2019. These numbers adjust for inflation every year.

Now, this is a very interesting credit because what this credit does, number one is to offset your taxes directly.

And the IRS says that 20 percent of the people that deserve this credit don't take it.

So, that's pretty interesting in and of itself.

The other thing that's interesting about it is that it's a refundable credit, which means that if you don't have enough taxes to use up the credit that you get, they'll actually send you a check for the difference.

So, you can theoretically get up to $6,300 back from the IRS.

They paid you for working.

There are also different education credits. They'll also pay you for continuing your education.

So, don't overlook these credits, because many people miss them. Again, any good tax planner can help you with this.

There are some ideas and tactics for the Smiling Retiree in the realm of saving taxes, both now and over your lifetime. How much you pay is truly in your control.

SPECIAL OFFER FOR YOU

People often ask me, "Hey, Navi, what should I do next?"

The answer is, "I don't know…what does "next" mean to you?"

The only way to know what it means to you is to have a conversation with a specialist, which is why I offer the Confidential Opportunity Conversation.

It's a great opportunity for you, and here are my three promises:

Number One: There won't be anything for you to buy.

Number Two: I'm usually going to be able to uncover at least two opportunities to either increase your income or reduce your taxes.

Number Three: You will know what to do next, if anything.

If you would like to schedule yours, give me a call at

630- 893-4142, or 715-845-4367.

I'd love to speak with you.

You can check for updates at www.NaviDowty.com

ABOUT THE AUTHOR
NAVI J. DOWTY, CFA ©

Navi J. Dowty, is a nationally-recognized Financial Educator, Best Selling Author, Speaker, and Retirement Income Planning Specialist, who has been interviewed on radio and TV, including NBC, CBS, FOX affiliates. Navi's insights (pronounced Navy) have appeared on multiple publications including, Forbes, Elite Advisor, Daily Herald, among others.

He is the owner of the tax planning and preparation firm, **DuPage Tax Group, Inc.**

This book, **Tax Secrets For The Smiling Retiree**, includes wisdom from over forty-five years of showing retirees, entrepreneurs, business executives and women on their own, how to reduce taxes, increase income and protect their hard-earned money from "wealth predators."

Navi has earned a top financial designation in the world achieved by less than 1%, and not held by more than 99% of financial advisors in the United States.

As a Financial Educator, he is a renowned speaker at events like the Harvard Business Expert Forum, NASDAQ, and the Leadership Speakers Forum at West Point; recently, he was sharing the stage with Legendary Astronaut, Buzz Aldrin.

He has shared his wisdom with the industry as a Continuing Professional Education Instructor and Expert Witness. Navi is the developer of the unique, trademarked *Smiling Retiree Process* ®, designed to help people optimize their wealth and save taxes.

Navi and his wife, Sue, enjoy life with their rescue dog, Molly, and spending time with their four children and four grandchildren.

APPENDIX

2019 Tax Rates

These will change every year

Taxable Income

Single

0 to $9,700	10 %
$9,701 to $39,475	12 %
$39,476 to $84,200	22 %
$84,201 to $$160,725	24 %
$160,726 10 $204,100	32 %
$204,101 to $510,300	34 %
Over $510,300	37%

Married Filing Jointly

0 to $19,400	10%
$19,401 to $ $78,950	12%
$78,951 to $168,400	22%
$168,401 to $321,450	24%
$321,451 to $408,200	32%
$408,201 to $612,350	34%
Over $612,350	37%

> A taxpayer is someone who works for the federal government but who doesn't have to take a civil service examination.   Ronald Reagan

Form 1040 (2018) Page **2**

Attach Form(s) W-2. Also attach Form(s) W-2G and 1099-R if tax was withheld	1	Wages, salaries, tips, etc. Attach Form(s) W-2			1	
	2a	Tax-exempt interest . . .	2a	**b** Taxable interest . . .	2b	
	3a	Qualified dividends . . .	3a	**b** Ordinary dividends . .	3b	
	4a	IRAs, pensions, and annuities .	4a	**b** Taxable amount . . .	4b	
	5a	Social security benefits . .	5a	**b** Taxable amount . . .	5b	
	6	Total income. Add lines 1 through 5. Add any amount from Schedule 1, line 22			6	
Standard Deduction for— • Single or married filing separately, $12,000 • Married filing jointly or Qualifying widow(er), $24,000 • Head of household, $18,000 • If you checked any box under Standard deduction, see instructions.	7	Adjusted gross income. If you have no adjustments to income, enter the amount from line 6; otherwise, subtract Schedule 1, line 36, from line 6			7	
	8	Standard deduction or itemized deductions (from Schedule A)			8	
	9	Qualified business income deduction (see instructions)			9	
	10	Taxable income. Subtract lines 8 and 9 from line 7. If zero or less, enter -0-			10	
	11	**a** Tax (see inst.) _____ (check if any from: 1 ☐ Form(s) 8814 2 ☐ Form 4972 3 ☐ _____)				
		b Add any amount from Schedule 2 and check here . . . . ▶ ☐			11	
	12	**a** Child tax credit/credit for other dependents _____ **b Add** any amount from Schedule 3 and check here ▶ ☐			12	
	13	Subtract line 12 from line 11. If zero or less, enter -0-			13	
	14	Other taxes. Attach Schedule 4			14	
	15	Total tax. Add lines 13 and 14			15	
	16	Federal income tax withheld from Forms W-2 and 1099			16	
	17	Refundable credits: **a** EIC (see inst.) _____ **b** Sch. 8812 _____ **c** Form 8863 _____				
		Add any amount from Schedule 5 _____			17	
	18	Add lines 16 and 17. These are your total payments			18	
Refund Direct deposit? See instructions	19	If line 18 is more than line 15, subtract line 15 from line 18. This is the amount you **overpaid** . .			19	
	20a	Amount of line 19 you want **refunded to you.** If Form 8888 is attached, check here . . . ▶ ☐			20a	
	▶ **b**	Routing number		▶ **c** Type: ☐ Checking ☐ Savings		
	▶ **d**	Account number				
	21	Amount of line 19 you want **applied to your 2019 estimated tax** . . ▶	21			
Amount You Owe	22	**Amount you owe.** Subtract line 18 from line 15. For details on how to pay, see instructions . . ▶			22	
	23	Estimated tax penalty (see instructions) . . . . ▶	23			

Go to *www.irs.gov/Form1040* for instructions and the latest information.

Form **1040** (2018)

Even if money could bring happiness, think what the luxury tax would be!

The reward for saving your money is being able to pay your taxes without borrowing.

A man pays a luxury tax on a leather billfold, an income tax on the stuff he puts into it, and a sales tax when he takes the stuffing out of it.

A fine is a tax for doing something wrong. A tax is a fine for doing something right.

Children may be deductible, but they are still taxing.

People who struggle with their income tax can be divided into two categories: Men and women.

Made in United States
Troutdale, OR
09/09/2023